DIAMONDS FROM THE ROUGH

By Erica Loberg

CHIPMUNKA CLASSICS

CHIPMUNKA CLASSICS

All rights reserved, no part of this publication may be reproduced by any means, electronic, mechanical photocopying, documentary, film or in any other format without prior written permission of the publisher.

Published by
Chipmunka Classics
United Kingdom

http://www.chipmunkaclassics.co.uk

Copyright © Erica Loberg 2017

ISBN   9781783823413

Supported using public funding by
ARTS COUNCIL ENGLAND

This is for you Dad

WE CAN BEGIN

What are you going to write about?
What are you going to write about?
You seem to be able to type on the liquid keys
Pretty well.

So

So

We can begin.

EXTREMITIES

Because nothing is ever
Enough
So where does that lead me…

Constantly bad.

GAINING COMMAND

Unfortunately texting started
As a median to connect
Or converse
And now it has become a
Strategic method
Of gaining
Command.

POEM POEM

Poem poem rhyme away
Poem poem
Find a way

To be commercial
And try to stay
Within the rules
Of writing schools

And utilize
Conventional tools
To be called a poet

That rhymes real cool.

THE RESTAURNT MANAGER

His ass was so wound up
That he didn't have to flex it
In his tight blue pants
Because those buttocks were ready
Without a squeeze
From his muscles.

His hair was blond
Tight shaved
Against his head
With a tiny Mohawk
Like a dinosaur bump on his brain
That ended with a flip
Of short bangs
That shot down
His face
Across his eyebrow
Making a new style for men
That wanted
A head full of hair.

He was a cross between a peacock
And tweedy bird.

He fluttered around the restaurant
With a tight thin tie
Slightly pulled down
So he appeared
To breath
While he bounced
Fiercely
Across the hard wood floors
Ready to
Rock and roll
The scene.

In pre dinner
Meetings

He clapped his hands
Like a school teacher
In a fifth grade classroom
To go over what he had gone over
474 times in his head
In his sleep
When he downed coffee
Because he's never touched
The free bread.

He's flawless
With absolute
Effort
Seeming like
There's none.

And some people are like that
And don't have to do squats
To get stone buttocks
To punch through their pants
Perfectly fitting the overall theme
Of easy perfection
And great hair
That was cut and teased
In early am hours
For hours.

A show
Of put togetherness
After meticulous effort
To be perfect.

Effort and nature
Together develop
Wanted perfection.

NEW YEARS TIME

New Years time
Are you mine?

Will you be
Beside me?

When midnight shines
Inside my wine?

Am I too late
To kiss you great?

My soul shall break.

SHE WAS A TIRED WOMAN

It was a Saturday morning
Not too early but
Early enough to
Stand over her ice tea
And put its cap on.

At the coffee bar.

In polka dot boxers
With a polka dot top
Straight out of bed
She was tired.

She was a tired woman.

SAVAGE

You eat and drink like a savagical fish.

WHAT IS YOUR POETRY?

Poetry is strange words
Beside each other
Covered with analogies that
Pump bizarre truths
Yet

Stand alone.

As not only different
But random
Are products of minds
Racing inside
Or caught in
A real time world

Where life walks at normal speed
And the progression
Of the mind
Flushes out
In a sentence

Of fierce thought.

Deep imagery
Quick through the
Juxtapositions of words
Manifesting the mind working
In different realms

Of the brain.

That is my poetry.

BARNEY'S BEANERY

A baby moth circles
A light at a bar.

A sticky counter
Reeks of stale booze
And dirty elbows.

Endless beers on tap
And deep thirsty tongues
Engulf pitches
Like water after
A five mile run.

A baseball game
Next to the kids in the hall
Baseball caps backwards
To the side
A tight crew cut hiding underneath.

A biker
His helmet at his feet.

A sexy blonde snake hips
Across the impromptu dance floor.

With pink cleavage
To each his own
She likes his superman shirt
And calves
His eyes walk down her chest.

Girls swirl in the mix
Flutter around.

Like moths to a flame
To sport brats hiding behind their claps
For their team
While sneaking a peek at the flesh
Of their counterpart.

HURRICANE

And the music played

And played and I heard it walking down the hallway
It flew kindly out of the door of the room

And there he was

The Champion of the World

My Dad

Sitting on his bed

Not ready to die

But ready to listen to Bob Dylan's Hurricane.

CAUSE SHE CAN'T WEAR RED

She had to take off her sweater
Cause she can't wear red.

You know you can't wear red
Anhhh
You know the rules
As she peeled it off
Underneath her sweater
Annoyed
Knowing how to take off undershirts
Easily
Without needing a private sector.

She put it on the table
And he took it.

You know you can't wear red
Oh you want my belt too?

She said
As she walked
Out the door
And grabbed her
Red belt
Ripped it from
Her waist
And now the school had her
Red sweater
And belt
Take it
Take all of it.

All her clothes
Were coordinated
And she was deeply frustrated
Which turned into pissed off
Thank God they didn't eye down
To her red shoes
Cause she couldn't possibly walk

In the halls
Or class with no shoes
And she walked away
From her fifteen year old ass sick with her outfit ruined
Cause it was red
And she should know better
Now with her top
Jeans with no belt
And her red shoes
That don't carry a voice
Cause she has nothing outside
Her clothes
To make it all work.

Fashion that was peeled on
Now shaked off.

Cause she can't wear red.

I WAS SITTING ON A BALCONY IN NEW ORLEANS

This is what it was like before it all turned to shit.

I was sitting on a balcony in New Orleans
At my best friend's house

He took the cover pic for my book
It rocked hard-core ninjas to the sky

Then I became someone else
Obviously someone in me

That went from sitting on that balcony
In my pink bra and boy shorts
Writing through the ongoing open crowd
Reading Lord Byron's poetry
When a homo neighbor
Holding a hurricane teasing his tonsils
Came up to me
And said

"Well hello dear."

That ended up with me walking around his place
It had a Pee Wee Herman paper plane
That hung from the ceiling
With a string to pull up and down
To make him fly
And a chandelier made out of plastic Barbie dolls.

Then it all went to shit.

I want someone to bring me back to that girl
With the plastic dolls
Falling from the ceiling
And my glittering dress
That spun out the title of my book.

Then somewhere, somehow, somewhy…

I went from the non-me
To
The me
Back

And it's gonna rock
Just as long as I
Keep it real
And not rest on
The past to
Justify my present

I was sitting on a balcony in New Orleans.

SEND AN EMAIL HERE OR THERE

Send an email
Wait for an email
Check here
Or there
Once an hour
Or day
Every two days
Then get a highlighted
Name
Popped out on the scene
You respond
As slow as possible
After time spent
Typing
Deleting
Saving as a draft.

Or you take it
In the time
You get it
And send whatever enters your mind
At that time
And place
Here or there.

Fear after sending
A rash email
Too late
To delete
That turns
To check your inbox
And see if there was
A response.

The name hits highlighted
On the screen
And you fix fear
With oh shit. Ok.

The fear of reading it ends with
Opening it.

Like holding your breath
And then starring down
That highlighted line
Of new mail
And after holding that breathe
You can breathe long and deep
And thankfully
Have oxygen running through your mind
When you open and read that email.

THE OSCARS ARE TOMORROW

The Oscars are tomorrow
Should I go to my parent's house?
Which is vacant, and watch it on the big screen
Or find a party
Filled with people who may be amused by my comments.
What the heck is that?
A feather, a boa, the wrong color, wrong size.
Yet I watch them
Every year.
I ran by Morton's today and saw the detour sign
claiming that Melrose at Doheny was closed for an event.
It's
The Vanity Fair party
The irony of that publication throwing such an event
Making cars detour
And I'm still wondering why I want to watch them walk in
And Ellen DeGeneres comedy
And best of
Show.
DeNiro never went
Against Hollywood giving gifts to themselves.
Yet the world watches
And gets into it.
So why do I?

WHISKEY

Hot breath
Open arteries
Kiss the moon
In an open rain
Whiskey.

SAN FRANCISCO

I'm going to SF

Tomorrow

Gonna see a show

Tomorrow

Gonna see my pals

Tomorrow

Gonne party late

Tomorrow

Gonna take a break

Tomorrow

Before it's too late…

WALKING IN HEELS

And it's not brief sigh of relief that I dodged a bullet this year.
That I managed to walk tic tic tic on the cement of the walk that you do
Always.
It sounds angry
Meaningful
Hardships in a heel
When really you just walk like a walker
Like someone that walks

But everyone has something to say about it.

Something.

CHRISTMAS DAY

Shower
Standing still
In the water
Glancing down the side
Of my body
My stomach
And down the beginning of my leg
And thought
When was the last time you've been in the shower with someone you were with?

I couldn't even think what it would be like
To stand naked
Honest
In the wilds of intimacy
Inside shower heated walls.

And it rolled down and inside my brain
And I wondered what is it like
To sleep in a bed with someone
Kiss someone randomly
While sitting nowhere
Doing nothing.

I held onto that thought
Maybe because I was high
But either way
It was Christmas day
I was in the shower
Alone
Wondering
How is the
Other life
And used floss to super clean my teeth
And I came back from my mind
And asked
Is it gone?
Thank god.
So you can't be hurt

But it's gone.

The need to not be alone.

And that's what I thought about in the shower
Then I got out my brand new blanket from Restoration Hardware
A present from my sister
For Christmas
And pulled out my dildo and masturbated
Like another of me
No other of me.
And went to sleep.
3
It was a surprise Sunday
Masked on Christmas.

THE REAL BARFLY

The real barfly
Doesn't leave the bar
Sits on the stool
Looks left and right
Back and forth
Right to left
The others
Don't necessarily come and go
But move in and out.

The barfly

Doesn't fly anywhere
Except from bar to bar
But when he lands
In there
That bar
He's there.

YOUR MESSAGE HAS BEEN SENT…GOOD BYE

Your message has been sent…goodbye.
After reviewing my message
Again
Sometimes again
Cause I get a kick
Out of my stomach
To hear my wondrous way of words
The juxtaposition
Metaphors
Plopping of ideas
In a sentence
It's not random
The mind breaks free of thought
And it comes out of your ass
It tells the mind
In its purest form.

Just like writing.

MAKE UP

And I put the mascara on.

With a dab of my previous day mascara
Almost in the hair
A little
In the lash.

I open the eye shadow chest
Eyes open to all
The colors
Sitting in padded pads.

As my eye scratches the palate of colors
I pick up my brush
And tantalize its course
Waving above the colors
Sparking in the seams.

I dip
Dab
And I dab my eyes
On the tip of my lids
To grab access sparkly dash shadow
On the page
Of my face.

And wonder if my eyelashes are worse than they were
Then when I put the mascara
On the lash
That already had day mascara
That did not want
To be interrupted.
Yet. But. Besides.
I reapplied.

And now I look like a clockwork orange
All over my drip drop
Tips
Of the lash.

A sun with a baton end for an eyelash.

AT SOME POINT

At some point
I hit a wall
My mind shrieks a great idea
And the ballpoint hits the paper
Empty
Then raises its head
Waiting
In frustration
For some thought
And the mind
Gives no release.

There is no needed relief
To finish the thought.

It's like getting really hard
Hard enough to squeal
Then stone walled.

White blank surfaces
Shines quicker than…

I sit longer than ever
Stuck in the weed haze
And have no answer to how the white shines
Quicker than…

WHAT KIND OF WORLD IS THAT

whether it's corporate america
or county tape

the everyman will be confined
stuck in cardboard walls
of a square frame
unable to think
out loud
with his own opinions
cause it's not easy
to hear the truth

truth

a void word
that is smothered
by the jefe
the man in the chair
behind the oak desk
while you sit there
inside red tape
and community refrigerators

there is no truth
inside the walls of
american business
cause you all
stand in fear

fear of having an opinion
fear of saying the wrong thing
fear of wearing the wrong hair clip
or wrong cascading colors
on a churchgoing tie

There is no truth
there is only a slow
death
of the soul
and spirit
trapped with nothing to do
in a stale computer screen
that is your world
what kind of world
is that?

POEM

I'm searching MY MIND TO WRITE SOMETHING
FOR SOMETHING OR SOMEONE OR
SOMETHING GIVING ME THAT
UNACKNOWLEDGED kiss of writing

That is not acknowledged cause no others can ever
know
The mind of a writer
Of a thinker
Of a pen speaker

No one
Unless
There is no unless

It's burning every moment on the fingertips of
communication.

SCREWED

When you're not a politician where does that leave you?

Screwed.

I've worked for the government in several facets.
I've seen the lackadaisical way of approaching work, or life.
You aren't gonna lose your job so, why not be a total mediocre individual in society.

Or, does the government pick people to work for them
That are fat and uneducated.

Let's feed into how we can continue to control the people.

If you don't hire people to think, or try or become something
Better
You're left with what we got:

Bull $##$ and zero work ethic to make some difference.

A group of government that is smart enough to hire idiots
And dumb enough to make agendas that feed those idiots
Is a sad statement.

That I will stand by.

WHISTLEBLOWERS WILL BE PROTECTED

I lost my job today
Or I was lost to my job
And stuffed in a corner

Whistleblowers will be protected.

I'm poised
I'm pissed that they put me in a cube
Outside a mailroom
Beneath binders of piles of paperwork
Angry binders
To read
To update
To do something in that item
To not earn a paycheck.

Whistleblowers will be protected.

It is all bullshit. Over and over and over again.
The same nothingness
Over and over till…

Noting happens cause it's in the
Bureaucracy of crap.

That's what people know
Bullshit on the page
On the premise
Of government

And there you have it.

Whistleblowers will never be protected.

PAIN

Pain.

It's easy when it's straight up
Like a flamingos left leg.

When it's long

It sits
In a hippos mouth.

The body forms back
When it's shaken.

                While the mind bleeds alone.

A Coy Reply To A Simple Mister

Just like Herrick upon his Julia's Breast
Or Marlow's Passionate Shepherd
Please have sex with me now
Or else we are wasting
Time talking on a date that we'll never have
That sets the precedence to have Raleigh
To make a reply
Ok you dirty nymph's reply to that shepherd
Let's just have love
Here and now
Love the leaves and trees and lands of nonsense
To escape the disturbance of lights
Let's just breathe into ourselves
Just like Herrick wants to suck Julia's tit
What's better than two minds meeting at the same bed
And make sure Marvell's followers copy my print
And write on about their own lovers
With a nod to those that glorify
Sexuality in its most beautiful carnivorous form
In poetry
And have the eye on the open hole

Of the woman poetess.

THE TRAVELER ON THE TRAIN

On the train
The camouflage makes one wary
Until you're in the ladies bathroom
Fighting for a sink
To clean the nasty smell of
Processed meat
Off your hungry fingers
Freedom and American food.

The soldier gets up
Off the train
Leaving some chairs
Open and
The traveler scoots over
And sits in the middle
To claim her space.

A child gets the go ahead
To sit down
When her mother pats
The empty seat
Beside the travelers space.

Her temporary pocket of
Seated relief
Now over
At the end of a tired day
She wanted away
From the alert child
Her happy laugh
Sitting upright
Clutching a bear
With its legs
Stretched out
Animation.

The traveler gets up
And moves down
A couple seats

More
Away from the youth
That's obliviousness
To solitude

The flee
Brought by a quiet child
With no deep breathing
Polluting her space
Or intrusive action
Bumping her territory.

She reads her picture book
Not aware that adults are restless baggage
Inpatient storms
Concealed in dry cleaning
The kid pops off
Her warm chair
Ready to go.

As the woman now sits
In between waiting bread
Who are ready to melt
Now
Stuck in a smelly line
Between puffy coats
The bulge in the seat
Squeezed in
Real tight
Like packed sardines
And the child steps up
To the sliding door
And springs off the train.

People want their space
And the child had a seat.

WHERE'S THE INSPIRATION?

Where's the inspiration?
I hung my little sister's ripped out sheet
Of shades, blocks of wonder.
The preparation of an artist
Few can see in an artist
Scratching pieces of their pencil
Carving
Spaces on a page into shadows.
It hangs beside me
On my green wall
Inspiration.

THAT KISS

I always remembered that first kiss
Rolling around in my mouth
And bed
For once
Chemistry eats everything
Two dancing bodies crossing spirits in a timeless mold
A loss of the self so strong that no thoughts interact
with reality outside
So intense you pull away
Dark motionless silence blinks
And you want more
You never forget
It's once in a series of men
And it's never planned but when it takes over
You hesitate that next time
After months it's almost a first kiss
So different you're not sure
But the anticipation sparks excitement
That wasn't there before
Because without the memory of the first kiss
The fire of ecstasy of a union tangled in arms falling
into each other
There's no point in knowing him.

ATTENTION TO DETAIL

Attention to the details
Of writing
In a text message
It's so misconstrued
Or hard facts
Across the diction
Of a meaning
Can be taken one way
When it's another.

I am interested in how the written work
Put together by words beside themselves
Makes a difference
In reading and
Interpreting information.

Some fly off emails
And it's not dissected
Or taken carefully.

It's just a sentence.
I think
Or think
In words
Every word makes a definition
In a sentence
And when some toss out words
From memories
Of their existence
Or words in ideas
And it's not fueled with meaning
From one's own born ability to construct
Or deconstruct sentences
And make them make meaning
It's a text without deep meaning
And thankfully a read passage that's just that
Reading

Without meaning.

MRS. HUGHES

A flower kisses the rim of her straw hat
Warm and cute.
Welcome to Drunk Driving School
La Di Da.
Matching pearls
Smiling across her chest
A suit that screams flamboyant citrus love
Hello, I feel your pain.
Wearing glasses with a gold rim.
"I don't want no drama."
Snaps in your face
Interruption reeks drama.
Drama is picking up your pen to sign in and open your mouth to ask...
"I don't need no drama."
Questions
Drama.
Standing still
Drama.
A smile
Drama.
Everything you do is wrong
Everything you don't do is wrong
Everything about you
Wrong.
She was a blond Barbie
She sashayed up to the window
With her bungee bands and pink lipstick.
Barbie thought she looked like a black Hallmark card
And said Hi.
"Get her out of here."
She pulled down her cropped top
What?
Good-bye.

GREY'S ANATOMY USED TO BE FUN

I'm watching Grey's Anatomy
And burst into tears.
The patient is undergoing cancer removal surgery and
"We'll know more once we go in there…there are
    things the lab tests can't detect."

Well great.

So that means tomorrow my Mom will undergo a
    surgery that tells us what
What's inside?
How bad it is?
Or isn't?

I run to the bathroom and wish I could puke
Like normal people when they are freaked out to the
point of revulsion
When they see a horrific car accident
Or are told they have an alien living in their stomach
But instead
My bowls barf out
Black diarrhea.

I feel better
And what comes tomorrow
Is.

A FRESH COAT OF PAINT

Wanting more
Typing with wet nails
Maybe almost dried
With the TV on mute
And your earphones
Inside your drum
Cause the 98-year-old guy
Next door
Can still hear
While thinking
About the next step
The next year
The purpose in your life
You are met
To meet
Typing carefully
On your Mac
Not sure if you are more worried about your black
finer moist nail polish
Or your silver Mac pro
Getting black nips here and there
On the keys
While you try to write
And the fingers stick to the center
Of the surface
Of the squares
And strange
And stupid
As it is
The rhythm picks up
Across the pad
Leaving the door
Open to the black paint
Permanently offending the keys
But you can't stop
Yet are careful
Of the polish
More so
Than the keys

The keys that spill your brain
Onto the screen
Priorities are strange
And forbiddingness is another thing.

WHOLE FOODS

It's an office for writers
Students
Looky lues
Internet gambling addicts.

A Mecca of computers
With people fighting for space
As they drop their bags in the seat
Beside them
As they fight for an outlet
For their dying computer.

They sit beside their food and plastic utensils
And you are roped in
Your seat
By technology
And foreign tongues.

You can't have a conversation
With your sister
And catch up on the latest TMZ gossip
Without someone nearby listening in
And making some face
As a means to find
Their way
Into your conversation.

There are bars of salads
And chicken swims in pesto sauce
While bread pudding melts at the dessert bar
Tantalizing your nostrils
And there is no stopping you from making the perfect syrupy portion
That you plop in a cardboard box.
The no nibbling signs warn the grazers
But doesn't stop you from picking grape leaves
And quickly popping them in your empty mouth
When the whole foods aprons
Are not looking.

The checkout line is like waiting for a rollercoaster ride
Line two lights up on the screen
Signaling that checkout five
Is ready.

But the system doesn't work
Because you're in line one
Waiting first
But in the queue
Somehow
You're last.

You can spend a whole day there and never leave.
Whole Foods
Whole paycheck
Whole Office
Whole Nation.

A BLUE TOOTH CAR AGAINST THE 70S

Is there a blue tooth in your car
Or a plugged in
Pandora
Streaming off your phone?
Fueling
Technology
Into your being?

Or

Do you have a bus
Or a train
Or an 8 track
Fueling your seams that are
Falling apart

In your Cadillac Seville.

BACK FENCE BAR

Not your normal neighborhood bar
Seven beers on tap
Neon signs
Attract lonely eyes
Wanting a Sierra Nevada

Packed with guys from Manhattan
And judgment takes the forefront
When Brooklyn lawns are unknown
Just a name
That is a notion
And a resume of
Livelihood
A scarlet letter on the chest
When you've committed no crime
But people think
Brooklyn's a sin
When they've never
Smelled the N train.

The bathroom smells of
Florescent acid flowers
Stenching down your back throat
With a lingering residue
It's the men's room
And there's no sign to differentiate
From the ladies
Because a curtain
Blocks the doorway to acceptance.

You get
A "talk"
From the asshole server
Curly haired bitch
As you bend down to respect her
And meet her eye to eye
Because you have to
Compete with thirsty customers
When she deserves a laugh
Across her face

With her condescending smack.

Where you want to dance
Like you own it
In a footloose bar
Where steps to the rhythm
Are desert storm
As your strapped to a chair
So beat your feet on the peanut shells
Scattered on the ground.

Tables of preps
Bob their heads
Singing their
Silent voices
Their own way
Because no one knows how they interpret
Ottis Redding
While the beat is kept
By the whistled lips
And rocking hips
Of the shoulders.

On tables of checkers
And peanuts
The crowds know music
Like sweet home Alabama
For guys in collared shirts
And girls in tube tops
Stir the crowd
Like a frat party guzzling beers
And never knew music outside the US of A.

Mr. West
A local hero
Throws peanut shells
On the ground
And he makes awesome
Waves of Fleetwood Mac
Hendrix
Many great chords
Smiling on the mic

And splitting the atom
On the strings
Of the guitar
Mouth open to the music
Closed eyed
Music maker.

The Back Fence.

SEARS

"You can see the sears building from here."
He said.

My Dad gave me those binoculars
As a house warming gift

He said
"This is why we won World War II."

I didn't know what he was talking about but
The binoculars were handed to me
And I took them looking for the
Sears building

I looked and
Saw a green sign.

I ended walking thinking

Thank God I am ready to write, once

Again

GENETIC GREATNESS

Silent beauty
That cries in the bathroom.

And is….
Fine.

Complexities make life unusual
And she takes herself for granted
Without knowing.

Like her free spirit
Her ability to adapt
Her genius
Her breast that loves
Another beautiful soul
Not yet known.

If only she had the knowledge of
The Tapped Greatness.
Of the mother
And daughter.

DANCING

Pockets of the imagination hit vibrations and shoot up
and dance
Outside their sphere of comfortable
And hit the sky with happy fists
Ready for the next ready breath for more
More
Dancing.

THE CALAMARI

Ronald was the Marlboro Man
For the Herb Leaf posters
Around the world.

He smoked every day
And only ate ice-cream with Betty
His wife.

We went to the Village Lantern
Ordered some beer
And calamari.

We chatted about their dogs
Their cats
Their latest dip in the ocean
And I watched the calamari
Slowly disappear
Off the plate.

There was one tiny calamari
Left hiding
Beside the lemon
That was squirted
To a death
The busboy picked up the dish.
"Wait!! There is still one more left!"
It was like a bomb went off
In Betty's insides
As she sprung up
From her chair
Pointing at the small squid
Like she had found a lost diamond.

She saw the reaction
Around the table
And sat back down.

"You have it."

She turned to Ronald
To end the embarrassment
Of jumping onto the plate
For the ten cents
She was going to eat
Since
After all
She paid for it.

Betty picked up her knife
And cut the dime in half
Leaving one for herself
And the other for her husband.

Betty had her half
Counted to ten
And thought it was fair game
To suck down
The other half.

No one in their bomb threatened seat
Was going to even consider
Taking it
But it was a kind gesture
To slice the noose in half
For her husband.

FREE FLOWERS FOR A LONELY WOMAN

Free flowers for a lonely woman
A day out of the earth.

Flowers like fresh donuts in a strip mall
Glazed and soft.

Open flowers stuffed up her nose
Like a child
Swallowing the donut down
8 minutes out of the oven.

The flowers safely
Stored
In her purse
After a few
Fell dead.

The mystery of the lonely rose
In her bag
Hurt and falling apart.

A child inhales the donut
And his stomach rips apart.

The child sinks their teeth
Into another soft sensation

As the flower drops dead.

Free flowers for a lonely woman.

MAN IN A WHEELCHAIR LOOKING FOR CHANGE

His one leg
Rolled out in front of
His tired wheel
Every time the light changed
His whipped out boot
Heeled its way forward
And dug
Into the ground
To get the wheels going
Before the light changed.

His cup was a prize
He won one night
Riffling through a trash can
Like a kid on Christmas morning
Who thrusts their fist
Down a stocking
Looking for that one gift
At the top of their list
That year.

Back and forth
The crosswalk
In and out
Of the cars
He knows his route
When the light will change
And at the end of his circle
Back to the street
When he raced against the
Dark yellow light
He gained enough momentum
To give his leg a break
And like a child
Weeee
Was back on the block
Waiting for the light to change
Again.

He was the man in the wheelchair
Making rounds
Around the stopped cars
Looking for
Change
For his cup
From his routine
From his cyclical
Life
On the wheel.

WHEN POETRY IS DEAD

Do you write until you die
Or until nothing's left

But isn't the death
The death of you
Losing your best friend
Losing your love
Losing your savior
Losing yourself
Poetry dead in me means

I'm dead.

SIGH

Oh to be
To be alone
Cool
And poise
Alone with him
And not all the shenanigans God darnet.

Why can't I just be cool smart
Without fiery spurs of thoughts
Running out all over the seams
While I am a cross between the real me
And the other real me.

It's hard to stop your real you
When your other real you
Thinks there's a difference.

The other real you is always the one that is right.
It monitors the real you
For the most part
But actually has no power
When you like him.

The real you pops out
Like popcorn
All over the bowls of the place
And the other self can only sit back
And roll it all over
In the mind.

Later
When things have calmed down
And you are driving home in your car
And rethink dialogue
That maybe means something
Or not
But you still play it in your head.

So stupid.
That the real self wins

Inside the chemicals of desire
And a deep breath
Cause the other real self
                    Can only sigh.

THE DISWASHER

It was the border separating
Mexico from California.
Those bandana hair wearing
Hard working guys
Were the backbones
Of the place.

The dishwasher
Was stuffed in the corner
With blue dishwashing gloves
Up to his armpits.

I didn't know if he could speak
For I never heard him talk.

When there was a mistake
And food was left for anyone
To grab
He was left
Sinking in dirty plates
And glasses
And all the meaning
Of the restaurant
Food.

I managed to be one
Behind the line
Trying to learn all the ingredients
In the five tacos
They offered me
I walked over
To the dishwasher
And handed him the plate
His washed out eyes
Starred back at me
Like I was the first human being
He'd ever met.

Probably the first human being

To befriend him
In the hole of
Dirty water
Firing away
All over his face.

He took the plate
And placed it behind him.

It sat there for over an hour
While he managed to hose
The avalanche of plates
Up to his chest.

Only after a break
From the rush
Did he get a chance to eat
His tacos.

Three tacos
Four hours later
Cold and soggy
And better every bite.

I HELD YOUR HAND

I held your hand
That's all I did
I tried to read the sports section but the room was too dark

You asked to see the sun before you died
I said
Dad it's too dark to read this March madness

And I held it
In silence

I had nothing to say
I knew he could hear me

I just held his hand
And when the nurse came it to fix a tube
In his throat
He flinched in uncomfortableness
And he squeezed my hand

I knew he was there
I knew he felt me
Holding his hand

Before he died

DANCING AT THE CLUB

She was at
THE CLUB.
With her girlfriends
Carving out a space
On the dance floor
With all the skinny bitches
That frequent the place.

Righteously
Strutting her hot red dress
Black heels
And gold rings.

She was not skinny
She was not LA.
She walked
On her unsteady heel
Ready and proud
And started dancing.

Gold shimmy
Around her legs
Pumping out of her
Hot flaming dress
That cradled her hips
She grabbed her waist
And swinging side to side
She danced.

Soft pedals on the ground
Carefully stopped some
And she pulled up her
Left shimmy
As she said

"You stopped dancing."

BOREDOME

Bored bored bored bored

To the point I can define it.

Boredom: The continual bursting of flaming thoughts
        with not enough to rapture it.

DO YOU HAVE MONEY FOR THE BUS?

His arm was thrown across his desk
His head rested on his shoulder.

She sat ready
The first to raise her hand.

He told his teacher
Screw you.

So they called his mom
To tell her
He had to go home
"He took my IPod."
He justified
When he lashed out
Like an angry child
When his pleasure
His escape
Was ripped
From his arms.

You got money for the bus home?
A blank shrug
So you want to go to school
With gangs and drugs
Or be here
Where you can get an education?
A blank face
Not sure what's the difference.

You should be in class
She said
Like it was an option
As he chilled on the bench
In the entry way
Doing nothing.

Confusion
Random kids walking around

Here and there
With classrooms some
Here and there.

And he sat in his chair
Slumped
With a kid
Behind him sitting
Tucked tight
In his chair
Smiling with thick glasses
And said
She's nice.

Out loud
A day
At a charter school
Do you know what a charter school
Is?

MIDNIGHT MISSION

I know about Midnight Mission.

There's a fire station in Skid Row
That goes off all the time
Morning
Noon
And
In the middle of the night

And it heads West to something elsewhere

Tonight there is a helicopter
Circling a building
In the heart of Skid Row

Something bad must have happened
Cause bad happen there
All daylong
And tonight it is something new.

I take out my binoculars and see the building.

It has a bright gold and blue sign
Of a person
With light coming out of his being
Like a rainbow of hope
Love
Help
And at the bottom
It reads

Midnight Mission.

I know about Midnight Mission.

It is death to any voice
On the streets
A place of theft
Dirty syringes

Unwanted sex.

So I wonder
What happened to that area tonight?

That the fire station that usually goes West
Goes East
Toward the mission.

It's not like there's anything new or different
There
Among the homeless
That sit the streets.

I wonder who came up with that sign on the building
of hope
Dreams
Gold lights screaming out of the mind of an image
That no one wants anything to do with

I wonder what just happened there

Tonight.

POETRY

And I guess that's how the story goes
There is a place
A mind
A heart
A soul
A person
Who lives and loves it.

Poetry.

A walking mechanism
To wake up the dead.
To steal the beauty
To learn your life
Your courage

Yourself.

WHISTLE

Is death a whistle?

A whistle that never blows
But it'll catch up with you
Death

The whistle of death
Will blow
On its own

Whether you keep it quiet
Or not
You can't avoid the face
The eyes
The ears
You can't deny the body
Death starts hard in the body
And from there

You gotta figure it out.

"EVERYTHING'S GONNA BE ALRIGHT"

"Everything's gonna be alright"
She wrote in her song.

I'm not sure if this is a love song or a self-love song
With a stripped soul.

Or a bad time that she sings herself through
Or delivers to her listeners.

I put it on to hear something
Then memory brings me back
To that day.

There is something to be said to lyrics that say

"Everything's gonna be alright."

It might
In love
In relationships
In life.

I walked down the decrepit streets of homeless today
With sheriffs to escort me
I felt like I had body guards
And shot the shit with them
About the streets
The drug deals
The mentally ill
The community that has been in existence
Since decades ago.

And what do we do with
Skid row?
Build high rises
Around to bring in the rich
To not appease the poor.

And we talked

The police
That knew everyone
With hugs and hellos
When a crack pipe gets whipped out
It gets a "No get that otta here."
As the crack smoker moves along
While a woman runs naked in the streets
And a drug dealer plays dominos beside a shelter
Bringing in cash from his street minions
And trash runs swirling around the streets
Like tumbleweed
Like it's normal
And people talk to the air
While a women's tits hang out over the trash filled sidewalk.

And they're not going

Anywhere.

Why would they?

They have their
Boom boxes
Their wheelchair friends
Their space
Their spot I guess you'd call it.

Some say to ship the homeless out
Another place
Mexico
A homeless village in Lancaster
You'd be surprise what people come up with
That walk the streets every day.

But homelessness doesn't move when it has a community

Here are the drug dealers
Here are the prostitutes
Here are the lost schizophrenic thinkers
That are at the disposal of all their life.

But…
"Everything's gonna be all right"
It was a song my best friend sent me to amend my soul
of bad times

And it brought my mind back
                      To that day.

THAT WE WERE AN US

Every time I look at the trash can
I watch the lid fall
And make sure at the end of the fall
It slows to a stop.

Cause I remember when we bought it
Together
At Bed Bath and Beyond.

For you.

Then it became ours.

Then you left
And the warranty on it is forever.

But not us.

Yet I look at it is every time it falls
For what?

To remember myself
That we had something
That you existed here.

That we were an us.

UNJILTED

You look at the patterns of your life

But for some reason you don't see them in your face

They tend to rot and rebirth
Again and again
In your mind
Your hard soft heart
Your unjilted soul

Cause the soul keeps you moving
Keeps you awake
Alive
Despite the turmoil of life
Hitting your chord

Sometimes the soul is the backbone of the chord of life

When really the soul is the only thing
We hold onto
That doesn't get jilted by life

It sings when it needs to
It soars beside you when you drown
It lifts the dark face
Off the mirror
And tells you a secret

I'll never let you get jilted
Your mine
And I'm yours
Forever

MEXICAN MEAT

You know you've had
Some real authentic
Mexican cuisine
When the lard
Around the meat
Hooks itself
In your back
Ivory stalk
And sits there

                Steadily.

BREAKFAST AT TORTAS, MURDER FOR LUNCH

"No drugs, No drug dealers, No loitering, No weapons, The Los Angeles police department makes regular and frequent patrols of this premises."

That's the sign outside my window when I look down to the street.

Tortas
Margaritas Restaurant Place
Tacos
Burritos
Y Mucho Mas!

Richard Ramirez
The night stalker
Used to eat breakfast
At Tortas.

The sign forgot to add…

No serial killers that have
13 counts of murder, 5 attempted murders, 11 sexual assaults and 14 burglaries.

Tortas
Open 24 hours a day

And a bag of ice is only 2 dollars.

I'll take my chances.

BOTTLENECKED

My body feels like a bottleneck

Zipped into an open glass

That I can't squeeze out of

                I'm Bottlenecked.

FACING YOURSELF

You see yourself
Every day.

Washing your chops
Lavering the creases
Beneath your eyes.

Or laugh line being formed
In
Your forehand
Or on the side

Of your smile.

And there lies the difference.

Which means

Facing yourself

Honestly

In the mirror

And saying

What?

Yeah that's right

What am I doing
What's going on
Why why

And if you're in that zone
You're lucky

Cause you're facing yourself

Across another self
In a mirror
That's you.

THE AMERICA NOW

Space for lease
213.555.1264

Not pasted to a building
Cause it probably costs
Too much

So it hangs on a flimsy nail
Blowing up and down
As the tides of the day
Change.

Space for lease is the
America now.

Let's not kid ourselves and say we're in the clear.

Our problems have just begun.

BEFORE THEY END

I want to play the music until it hurts
But the earphones don't go up that high
Even when I take mercy
On the neighbors
And use no speakers
To fuel my desire
Need to pulse myself
In music
Even then
With the earphones
In my brain
It's still something more
It must be like a bad drug
That's good
Music versus nightmare.
Where does this poem come from?
Why does it come through my skin so easy?
Easier than thinking about putting the seat up
Or down
To go to the bathroom.
It sits so easy in the chair.
Easy is not planned
And it's still good
It's hearing music in the lens of hearing
And makes it that much better.
It's still not flowing
Or thought of
Or thinking of
It's a clear comfortable plug moving
Too fast
To determine
Where it's at
But it makes itself apparent
With the result.
A mixture of music
Careful typing on the keyboard
And sentences
That you don't know
Before they end.

THE NEVER WOMAN

It sat on the floor outside my loft
Cause I locked myself out

And waited for the key lady to
Let me in

And somewhere between glancing down the hall
And taking an annoyed breathe

It hit me.

It has to be about you
Be the man cerebrum

And you might just surpass that gender.

HOW DO I DO IT DIFFERENT?

What if I just act

More than before
Or what I know

Cause what I know
Isn't making it

Action makes production
Progress

Not always.

So where does that leave us

Sleeping in
Eating out
Staring at an orange moon

While bouncing an
Electric leg
Beneath your desk.

Action is progress

If it's found right
And poured right

But we might continue to hit a wall in the sphinx of

What else do I have to do

To make it?

UNTITLED

So you chalk up an old love
With an old friend

Music

That brings you back
To the mind

And it sinks
Inside your bodily form

And the mind rests unsteady

Cause those songs
Bring you back
To something

And whether it's good
Or bad

Your body eventually finds itself

And carriages the mind

That you want to forget.

HIS SHIRT ON YOUR BACK

You pull it up
To your nose
Breathing him in
His soap
Detergent
Cologne
In soft
Smooth folding threads
Foreign to your face
Wishing your lungs
Could take in
Just more
Before you
Have to
Stop and regroup
Thirsty lungs
Till you return
Again
To your pleasure.

A mix of clean lust
Like soft butter
You pull it up
Once more
And try to choke
Back the smell
To stamp it
Deep in your throat
But it's always fleeting
Till you
Catch the next wave
Like a smooth drug
Running deep
In your blood.

In each possible thread
The neckline
Cuddles your nose

Straining
Your breath
Wishing it could
Take in more
Your sense newly accustomed
To his smell
Takes a lesser scent
The next time
But still a breath of himself
Your memory of the night
Of rash bodies
That cupped each other's skin
And rubbed
Against each pore.

That muffled smell
You can never remake
Or bottle
So are left with a day
Before your flavor engulfs
The state of his memory

From the night before.
It's the shirt that you wear
On the way home
A relic of the night
That might bring him back

That smell left on your back
Fading each sniff
Not knowing till more

If any.

FORCE FEEDING

I force feed
Poetry

Down your lips

That seal
Unopened

To the life
Of life

Of poetry.

SO MUCH

Would I have a different life if my brain didn't meet the world
So much
So fast
So all the time
That every second has to be filled.

Every   second   has   to   be   filled

Or else

Toxic things happen

CYNICISM

There's too many instances
Of too many great things
To be such a cynic.

Somehow
I will bury myself
Up
From the madness and find…

MY COUNTY NON-JOB

Today is like any other day
I remain in my mindless
Hole
Of a cubicle computer
Waiting to go
Wherever they plan to throw me
Out onto the street
Out of a job
Out of this place
Where the only thing left
Is the slow death
Of lacking freedom.

PERCEPTIONS

Our hearts fall deep
In our gut
And on our soft arms
Under the flesh.

And when you live
Like that
With that
Such piercing reality
You have to step back.

You have to create a barrier
But that's bullshit
Because regardless of our ability
To numb
Or isolate
Or pontificate strength
We will always be
Hit by our insides.

It is human nature
To decide if you are going
To bear arms
Or stand naked.

Some that bear arms
Don't know they are actually
Lashing out
Like a frightened beast

That knows too much
About life
So are themselves.

Others...you cry
We cry a lot
And wait for those times
When we're not diving
Deep inside
And not aware
Of everything.

Those times that we are free to enjoy life.

Life. It's your. Perceptions.

ERGONOMICS

Ergonomics
So stupid
Sitting in a bored to hell
Training
On

Ergonomics

How to sit right
How to organize your pens
Your papers
Your chair
Your office suck life.

When you hate your job
Does it really matter if your keyboard sits right
On your piece of shit desk?

Ergonomics

Bleed to death before
The next training hits

Next week.

HOW DO I WRITE A RAISON IN THE SUN

How do I write a raison in the sun?
Or a Poe's *Raven*
How 'bout a Ginsberg *Howl*

How do I write a poem
To put me on the map

A howling raven in the raison sun.

I SHOULD, BUT I DON'T

I feel the same
I feel like I would otherwise
No difference

I should feel something
I should hear something
From my heart

I should
I should I should

But I don't.

I'm just the same.

I'm drinking water out of the water club bottles
At work

I'm saying oh I'm sorry
When someone runs into my path

But

I'm driving my Vespa
And see a hard orange light
Racing against the red
And would normally stop
But
Keep going

What do I expect
Out of myself?

Stop my Vespa through a hard orange
Sit down to a coworker and be sad

Be angry and rude when people get in my way
On the street?

There are a lot of things I could be
With total righteousness

But I don't

And it worries me

I should, but I don't.

I hear bad news
And I just keep on
Checking my email
Writing stories
Living my same life.

I wonder when the hard orange light
Will be a sign
That it's not okay.

Will make me stop
Like it did before
I heard
You were dying

So I'm a little worried
I feel the same

But acting different

Slightly.

AND IT'S THAT SIMPLE

And it's that simple

Pull up the imagnet to the world of
Fingers knocking on a screen

A society that taps a screen as a means to survive

Cause most can't live without their blackbruise
Or imacaholic

So we are left thinking it's easy
Simple
Bounty

When really it's just a leap toward
Non human contact

Across the Internet world
And inside the streams of
Those that still want to retain

Human contact

Outside a screen tapping sphere.

4 SEASONS

Winter Winter
Almost gone
Winter Winter
Here's my song.

Cloudy rains
And snowy flakes
Will sit back
For spring to break.

Spring Spring
It is here
Spring Spring
Here's my cheer

Flowers bloom
And showers wait
For summer to come
Take its place.

Summer Summer
Soon to sing
Breaking waves
In oceans dreams

Sunny days kill the sky
Till autumn
Brings a tune to sing

Seasons Seasons
Always change
And leave an imprint

On my brain.

ZERO

Without my writing
What do I have?

Zero means to handle reality
Zero means to breathe
Zero means to survive

Zero Zero Zero.

THE DIVORCE

Divorce is a wary crime
When the children
Don't see it's time

To end the
Tug and pull
And silent blows
That parents hold

Till it's too late
It's time to break
And children scream
Inside their dreams

If only they knew
It's better to be raised
With two parents separate

Then both in rage.

SILENCED LOVE

I love your lips
I love your eyes
I love everything about you

If only I could tell you
Why.

IS THIS ON?

Her nails were bright red
She dabbed them over the heater
And said it wasn't on.

And the Korean woman yapped in their language
With their soap opera on
In the background.

Yap yap
They were saying what?

"It's not on."
She asked in a statement
Yap yap
"The light is on but it's not on. The heater."
They walked over to adjust it
And she was content for a few minutes.

"When will they be dry?"

No answer.

She had a fur coat on
On a hot spring LA afternoon
And tired
Ruly skin
And perfect red nails.

She fell asleep with her nails under the dryer
Then woke up

"I fell asleep."

"When will they be dry?"

THIS WHICH HAS NO NAME

My father died
And I think he's alive

I see a text come in
And think it's my Dad

I listen to Waylon Jennings
And I start to cry

THANK GOD!!

Finally I feel something
It feels good

Better then walking through life
Same old shit
Same old thoughts…

Just not about this

This which has no name.

THE HOPE…THE DREAM…THE REALITY

My hope was to write a book to open people's eyes
To educate
To enlighten
To be a springboard to
Advocate change.

My dream was to open a dialogue
To take down the walls of silence
To stop the fears of the unknown
To give a voice for those that don't.

My reality is I got zipped up
Made silenced by those not willing to take the baton
Of hope
And dreams.

Instead you killed the hope to make the dream

A reality.

STORM OF MADNESS

Storm of madness
Never dies

Storm of madness
Has its pride

Storm of madness
Has a face

Storm of madness
Finds its place

Storm of madness
All alone

Storm of madness
Welcome home.

SOOOO IMPORTANT

Like it's so important
You fake phone calls
From men you don't know.

You fake cocktail parties
So you can stop by in a slutty dress.

You fake a lot

Is it that important?

Yeah, actually
It is.

THAT GRIN

And then one day you realize

You'll always be you
With a grin on your sleeve
Cause you should
Know better

But you don't.

THAT'S HOW HARD

You won't let me in.

And I've tried

      And

           tried

                And

                      tried

In every way

You never want to ever speak of again.

That's how hard I tried.

THE EMERALD

She's a voice of kindness
And wrath
She's a voice of strength
And denial
She is the strength unknown
That you'd ever know
With a quick glimpse
Or shocking face
That said
Excuse me
She has green eyes
And a bright smile
That resonates across the boards of
Civilizations
And you are lucky to see it
Or even know it
You are damn lucky to be in the presents
Of such an
Emerald.

SUFFOCATED

I feel suffocated
When my temporary watch
Cups my wrist
Like a noose
Around a layer
Of skin.

I hate that feeling of confinement.

Like your eager
Ready to give me a kiss
Need
With a tangerine smile.

I don't like the way you
Have to
Kiss me
So desperate
In the morning

Like you never get the chance.

OF YOUR LIFE

Just write
Just write
Just write

That's all you have
To save you from

The
Oblivion

Of nothingness.

LIPSTICK

Her lipstick was like the kind you played with
In your mother's medicine cabinet
Where she kept her free bags of goodies
That she got
When she bought over a hundred dollars
Worth of bait.

Lipstick
Pasted across her thin lips
Crooked but sure
When it was smeared on
And smacked across her teeth
Leaving red lines across her gray sticks
Radiant.

Lipstick
Pops open
And the words
Dribble out
Moist
Cut from the thick stick
The words hang in the air
And bleed as they cross the red gate.
The top right side lip
Curls up
And the bottom lip
Grabs it to seal the next word.

Lipstick
Her life jacket in the Dead Sea
To mask the speech
Of aging.
Her best friend in the mirror.
A reminder of youth.

The innocence of aging
Caught in the same old stick
That her mother used
And she shared
When she wanted age
On her lips to seal innocence.

Now wants to seal age.

DIAMONDS FROM THE ROUGH

There was a box on the table in the middle of the living room

A brown box
I assume
I don't know
I wasn't there
When my sister opened it
Wondering what was in
It

She said it looked like crystals form some
Mediterranean Sea

It was my father's ashes

Sitting in the middle of the living room
In a box
Locked up in a zip lock bag

He was sitting on a table… in a box… inside a plastic bag

How long or how or why
I don't

I wonder what my Mom knows

PENS IN A CUP

I fire through every pen in my stacks upon pen
between a pens dream
Yet I never have a pen
Or ever touch those stems of blue ink
Sitting in a cup on my desktop
Pulling off cap of caps of caps to more caps of a pen
and the paper scribble
Scribble
It's another pen
That doesn't work right out of the bat
Cause it is new
And old in the cup
Every pen top popped off and hits the paper.
Scribble after three rounds of wings
To make the ink strike the paper in between a circle
On the paper.
Pen and pull
Draw
Keep stringing circles of quick blue butter.

Another pen
And another
And a thrust of a different circle pumps through the
veins of the pen
That new pen
Outside the cup
Now sitting beside the twelve others fleshing
themselves out on the notebook paper.
The ink slow to paper….
Makes the next pen outside the whole cup worth it
And after
All the pens.

www.ingramcontent.com/pod-product-compliance
Lightning Source LLC
Chambersburg PA
CBHW031450040426
42444CB00007B/1039